Kids on Track Checklists

Written by
Michele L. Fitzsimmons
MA-Reading Teacher & MA-Counseling
with
M. Theresa Bromley, PA-C,
MHS-Physician Assistant

The Parts You Don't See
Written & Illustrated by
M. Theresa Bromley, PA-C,
MHS-Physician Assistant

authorHOUSE®

AuthorHouse™
1663 Liberty Drive
Bloomington, IN 47403
www.authorhouse.com
Phone: 1-800-839-8640

© 2010, 2011 One Sweet World, Inc. All rights reserved.

No part of this book may be reproduced, stored in a retrieval system, or transmitted by any means without the written permission of the author.

First published by AuthorHouse 06/03/2011

ISBN: 978-1-4520-9213-3 (e)
ISBN: 978-1-4520-9212-6 (hc)
ISBN: 978-1-4520-9211-9 (sc)

Library of Congress Control Number: 2010915743

Printed in the United States of America

This book is printed on acid-free paper.

Certain stock imagery © Thinkstock.

Copy Editor - Denise Ciraldo
Cover Design - Carol Kalfian
Cover Illustrators - Alexis Bromley and James Fitzsimmons

Content available as a smartphone application
visit www.kidsontrackchecklists.com

Because of the dynamic nature of the Internet, any Web addresses or links contained in this book may have changed since publication and may no longer be valid. The views expressed in this work are solely those of the author and do not necessarily reflect the views of the publisher, and the publisher hereby disclaims any responsibility for them.

www.kidsontrackchecklists.com

As with a plant, so with a child. His mind grows by natural stages. A child creeps before he walks, sits before he stands, cries before he laughs, babbles before he talks, draws a circle before he draws a square, lies before he tells the truth, and is selfish before he is altruistic. Such sequences are part of the order of Nature...Every child, therefore, has a unique pattern of growth, but that pattern is a variant of a basic ground plan.

(Bigge and Hunt, 1962, p. 166)

ABOUT THE AUTHOR

      Michele Fitzsimmons lives in Yorktown Heights, New York, with her husband and three sons. She graduated from New York University in 2002, with a master's degree in counseling. She was a school counselor and reading teacher at PS 156 in the South Bronx, New York. In 1999, Mrs. Fitzsimmons received a master's degree in teaching reading and writing from Manhattanville College. She has taught first grade in Katonah and Harrison, New York. She is a New York State-certified reading teacher and elementary school teacher, and earned a bachelor's degree in early childhood education in 1996 from the University of Delaware. She grew up in Chappaqua, New York.

www.kidsontrackchecklists.com

ABOUT THE AUTHOR

M. Theresa Bromley, a native Chicagoan, currently lives in Mahopac, New York, with her husband, daughter, and son. After graduating from Loyola University Chicago with a BS in biology, Theresa earned her master's degree in health sciences and physician assistance from the University of Medicine & Dentistry of New Jersey. She has been practicing hospital-based pediatrics since 2002, and has focused on neonatology since 2007. Mrs. Bromley is currently a neonatal Physician Assistant for the Danbury Hospital Newborn Intensive Care Unit in Danbury, Connecticut.

The greatest way to secure our future is to nurture our children. We dedicate this book to the parents and caregivers who foster the growth of the children they love.

www.kidsontrackchecklists.com

CONTENTS

Introduction	**1**
The Parts You Don't See –	
a short story	**4**
How to Use This Book	**15**
Kids on Track: The Checklists	
Birth-3 months	**22**
3-6 months	**27**
6-12 months	**33**
1-2 years	**39**
2-3 years	**47**
3-4 years	**55**
4-5 years	**65**
5-7 years	**74**
7-11 years	**86**
Early Intervention Phone List	**97**
Acknowledgments	**99**

INTRODUCTION

I decided to write this book because, when I needed it, I searched for it and could not find it.

When my son was 15 months old, I noticed that he wasn't really walking and said only the word "up" in reference to everything. What would any parent do? I looked for a book. Unfortunately, I could never find one that answered all my questions. I wanted to know specifically what behaviors and skills to look for at each age.

Having taken numerous psychology and education classes for my career development, I was familiar with the ages-and-stages theories from the major psychologists in the field. So I pulled out my textbooks and began referring to the developmental charts.

After realizing that my suspicions were valid and that my son was delayed in both language and physical development, I spoke with my pediatrician. He gave me the phone number for Early Intervention Services (EI) in my area.

So I called my local EI center, discussed my concerns, and was scheduled for an evaluation. My son was tested in three developmental areas: physical, educational, and language. Three different therapists came to administer the evaluation on three different days. These therapists were friendly, and my son thought he was "playing" during the sessions.

The results of the evaluations confirmed that my son was delayed in two area: physical and language. He would need to receive language services twice a week and physical therapy once a week. These services would be provided in my home with each session lasting 45 minutes, and all materials would be supplied by the therapists.

Naturally, I was nervous about having someone in my home, and about how my son would react to the therapists. But, to my surprise, he bonded with them immediately. They were personable and professional. It was like having a private teacher in my home while I took care of daily chores.

Within a few weeks, I saw improvements. He was using more sign language to communicate, his vocabulary grew, and he began to walk. By the time he was 3 years old, he tested out of early intervention and no longer required their services. Today, my son reads above his grade level and is age appropriate in all developmental areas. In my case, my son received the help he needed to get him where he is today.

Hence, the purpose of this book is to help parents determine if their child needs help and get the necessary assistance, but without the anguish I experienced. Having gone through this, I know that when you suspect your child has a delay, a lot of unpleasant emotions are involved: guilt, confusion, sadness, helplessness. It is important to realize that these feelings are normal and that resources are available, such as teachers, pediatricians, and now this book.

DID YOU KNOW THAT...?

- There are 5 main areas of child development: Thinking, Social, Moral, Language, and Physical.
- Each of the 5 main areas continues to develop from birth through adulthood.
- Every state has Early Intervention Services (EI) to help your child if he or she has significant delays.
- EI evaluations are free. Just call your state EI center. A list of EI numbers referenced by state is included in the index located at the back of this book.
- This book was written to help you determine whether or not to make that call.

Let's take a closer look at the five main areas of development, by reading the following short story, *The Parts You Don't See*.

www.kidsontrackchecklists.com

The Parts You Don't See

A SHORT STORY ABOUT
YOUR CHILD AND DEVELOPMENT
By M. Theresa Bromley, PA-C,
MHS-Physician Assistant

I'd like you to meet this

newborn named Jamie.

The day Jamie was born,
a mother was worn and
a father was awed by his baby.

www.kidsontrackchecklists.com

Physical

Mommy, Daddy, do you know there are many parts to me? You can help me grow the things you cannot see.

Language

Thinking

Moral

Social

Physical Development is how my body interacts with and learns from my environment.

www.kidsontrackchecklists.com

Language Development is how I communicate with others.

Thinking Development is how I gather the information I need to act with purpose, to think with logic, and to manage my environment.

www.kidsontrackchecklists.com

The Parts You Don't See | 12

Social Development is how I interact with others and develop my ideas about myself.

Moral Development is how I learn to view my choices and the effects of my actions with regard to myself, my community, and my environment. This is how I learn right versus wrong and learn to understand the rules that shape my behavior.

www.kidsontrackchecklists.com

So feed me, love me,
And watch me for
delay...

But please relax.
And remember, I will
be okay.

How to Use This Book

I have created user-friendly checklists in five areas of child development: thinking, social, moral, language, and physical. These checklists are an accumulation of my decade of teaching experience, graduate-level child psychology coursework, my interaction with early intervention services, and my experience in raising three boys. These checklists will guide you to track your child's development and identify possible delays.

According to the New York State Early Intervention Program regulations (10 NYCRR 69-4.1 (h)), "Developmental delay means that a child has not attained developmental milestones expected for the child's chronological age adjusted for prematurity in one or more of the following areas of development: cognitive, physical (including vision, hearing, oral motor, feeding, and swallow disorders), communication, and social/emotional" based on the NYS EI criteria. In New York, a child receives services when the evaluation determines "a 33% delay in one functional area or a 25% delay in each of two areas." What does this mean? For the purpose of this book, developmental milestones have been collected from multiple sources and written in plain language to help you easily determine if your child may need an EI evaluation.

Kids on Track Checklists is divided into age categories with key milestones listed in each of the five areas of development. **Check off the skills as they**

www.kidsontrackchecklists.com

happen and use the activities suggested to help your child master these skills and behaviors.

Keep in mind that if more than a few items remain unchecked in one or more of the development areas over time, this is a red flag to think about calling for an evaluation. Here is a simple guideline:

- 1/3 of the skills in at least one area are NOT checked off.
- This gap in skills appears over two age stages.

If your child meets the above criteria, consider calling your state EI number listed in the back of this book as a first step.

Here's an example.

Imagine a child is 18 months old and only uses hand gestures and body language to communicate. The child responds to his name, points to some body parts, points at pictures in a book, and listens to rhymes.

Please refer to the sample checklists on the following pages that illustrate this scenario.

At 1 year of age, the following items were checked off on the list.

> **6-12 months**
>
> ## LANGUAGE DEVELOPMENT
>
> X Waves and holds up arms for communication
> __ Vocalizes to get/keep adult's attention
> X Responds to his/her name; e.g., baby Jamie becomes excited when asked, "Where's Jamie?"
> __ Imitates some adult speech sounds
> __ Babbles using longer sounds; e.g., babababa, mamamama
> __ Knows/speaks a few words

> **1-2 years**
>
> ## LANGUAGE DEVELOPMENT
>
> X Listens to simple rhymes and stories
> X Points to a few body parts, if asked; e.g., eyes, nose, and mouth
> X Points to pictures in a book, if asked
> __ Makes many word approximations; e.g., "da" for "cat" or "nana" for "banana"
> __ Categorizes; e.g., says "doggie" for all animals
> __ Uses more words every month
> __ By age **18 months,** uses about 50 words or approximations of words
> __ By age 2, uses about 150 words or approximations of words
> __ Starts using 2-word sentences

    In this example, a call for an early intervention evaluation is appropriate. In the 6-12 months age stage, at least 1/3 of language skills are absent because 4 of the 6 items are **not checked off.** In the 1-2 years age stage, there is evidence of a gap in language skills because 4 of the 7 items appropriate for this 18-month-old are **not checked off**. Again, when considering an EI call, we are looking for 1/3 of the skills left unchecked.

If you find that your child is not exhibiting the behaviors or skills listed in the appropriate category:

- Use the *Activity Boxes* in this book to help your child master any missing skills.
- Consider contacting your local EI center for a free evaluation. (See the list of EI phone numbers at the back of this book.)

If your child is in school, ask the teacher if he or she has the same concerns. Next, keep your pediatrician informed. Finally, use the checklists in this book.

A key stage is the 1st to 2nd year. At 18 months, review the checklists. **Remember, the stage is more important than the age.** You are looking for the progression and the movement through the stages. Finally, go with your instincts. ***If you have a concern, you should address it.***

If you decide to contact Early Intervention Services, begin with the phone list located at the back of this book. The numbers, listed by state, are intended as a starting point. Armed with the information gathered from the checklists, you will be ready to discuss your child's situation.

If you decide to call and are unsure of what to say, a good way to start the conversation is as follows:

"Hi. My name is ___. I have concerns about my child's development and would like an evaluation."

You will be directed from there.

www.kidsontrackchecklists.com

Please remember that an evaluation is a good thing because you will know your child's skill level in the major areas of development. This is great information to have about your child!

This book will help you track development and identify potential delays. In a busy world, it is essential to have an easy-read, go-to guide for monitoring child development.

Disclaimer

The author of this work has used her academic studies in the field of child development as well as her practical experience as a teacher and as a mother to develop the charts and information contained in this book. She has also checked her conclusions and findings against other sources that she believes are reliable in their study of child development.

However, in view of the possibility of human error or changes in child development theory, neither the author, nor any other party who has been involved in the preparation or publication of this book makes any warranty that the information contained herein is, in every regard, complete or accurate, and they disclaim all responsibility for any errors or omissions or for the application of the information contained in this book. Parents are encouraged to consult with their physician or with a child-development expert in reaching any conclusions on their child's development.

Kids on Track

The Checklists

What my child should be able to do and when

www.kidsontrackchecklists.com

BIRTH - 3 MONTHS

THINKING DEVELOPMENT

__Looks at caregiver's face while feeding
__Watches caregiver's mouth when talking
__Fixes eyes on high-contrast objects, such as faces and black-and-white objects
__Looks at own hands and feet
__Reacts when caregiver is out of view; e.g., becomes fussy
__Becomes active when shown a toy; e.g., flaps arms and legs
__Follows objects with eyes about a foot away from face
__By 3 months, reaches toward toys

SOCIAL DEVELOPMENT

__Seeks bottle or breast at predictable times
__Sleeps well when put down regularly in a quiet environment
__Responds positively to affection and attention; e.g., makes eye contact during playtime

MORAL DEVELOPMENT

See Age 2

www.kidsontrackchecklists.com

LANGUAGE DEVELOPMENT

__Recognizes mother and her voice
__Cries and coos
__Cries vary for different needs; e.g., the sound and frequency of the cry will be different for hunger vs. being tired

---

Birth-3 months Activity Box

THINKING DEVELOPMENT
- Hold soft, black-and-white toys 8 inches from baby's face and slowly move object from side to side.
- Face baby toward shadows on walls, or ceiling.
- Face baby toward spinning objects, such as pinwheels or fans.

SOCIAL DEVELOPMENT
- Commit to a 3- to 4-hour feeding schedule to establish consistency.
- Follow a cycle of eat, sleep, and play.

LANGUAGE DEVELOPMENT
- Listen for different cries to better understand baby's needs.

PHYSICAL DEVELOPMENT
LARGE MUSCLES

__Sucks when cheek or mouth is touched
__Touches face with hands
__Turns head to each side while on stomach
__Lifts face, and eventually head, while on stomach
__Attempts to crawl while on stomach
__Turns head to each side while on back
__Brings hands together in front of chest
__Throws open both arms and legs while on back
__Kicks at toy with feet

SMALL MUSCLES

__Closes and opens hands
__Makes a fist with both hands
__Grasps a small toy

Birth-3 months Activity Box

PHYSICAL DEVELOPMENT
- Put a finger or small toy in baby's hand to encourage grasping.
- Provide baby with supervised stomach time to help develop neck strength and prepare for crawling.
- While baby is on stomach, put a toy on one side and then the other, to encourage head rotation.
- While baby is on stomach, dangle a toy slightly above eye level to encourage head lifting.
- Clap baby's hands during playtime.
- Place your hand or a toy at baby's feet to promote kicking. This can be done while baby is lying on back or on stomach.

3-6 MONTHS

THINKING DEVELOPMENT

__Smiles at familiar voices
__Recognizes name by turning head when name is called
__Looks for dropped toys
__Watches caregiver walk across the room from a few feet away
__Stares at and plays with toy in hand
__Bats at dangling objects; e.g., stroller toy
__Reaches for a small toy from a short distance away
__Reaches for food
__Reaches for self in a mirror

SOCIAL DEVELOPMENT

__Smiles when smiled at
__Moves eyes in direction of familiar voices
__Smiles or laughs when played with

MORAL DEVELOPMENT

See Age 2

3-6 months Activity Box

THINKING DEVELOPMENT
- Place baby on a clean mat under dangling toys, such as an activity mat.
- While baby is on stomach, place toys just out of reach to encourage moving and grabbing.
- Place a toy mirror near baby.

SOCIAL DEVELOPMENT
- Play peek-a-boo game.
- Smile close to baby's face to encourage baby to smile back.
- Call baby's name when you are out of view to promote head turning.

LANGUAGE DEVELOPMENT

__Begins babbling; e.g., baba, papa, mama
__Gurgles and laughs
__Makes sounds when excited or unhappy
__Responds to tone of mother's voice
__Pays attention to music and toys that make different sounds

---

3-6 months Activity Box

LANGUAGE DEVELOPMENT
- Repeat baby's babbling sounds; e.g., "ba ba ba," as conversation.
- Use consistent voice tones; i.e., high or low, to communicate with baby.
- Place baby near toys with buttons for sounds and music.
- Exaggerate laughing during play.
- Play a variety of music.

PHYSICAL DEVELOPMENT
LARGE MUSCLES

__Holds head up while on stomach
__Pushes up with hands to raise chest
__Controls head position when seated with or without support at waist
__Sits steadily briefly
__Lifts legs
__Holds feet with hands
__Pulls feet to mouth while lying on back
__Rolls sideways, stomach to back and then back to stomach
__Bounces on feet when supported in a standing position
__Kicks each leg independently while on back

SMALL MUSCLES

__Holds bottle or breast with one hand and then both hands
__Shakes toys
__Holds objects first with palm and fingers only and then adds the thumb
__Claws with hands to get toys
__Keeps hands open more frequently; i.e., instead of fists

3-6 months Activity Box

PHYSICAL DEVELOPMENT
- During play, lay baby on stomach and hold toy out of reach. When baby is tracking toy with his/her eyes, slowly move toy behind baby to help him/her roll from stomach to back.
- Starting in back-lying position, hold out fingers for baby to grasp and encourage him/her to sit up.
- Sit baby up, for short periods of time, in an age-appropriate baby chair.
- Briefly hold baby in standing position.
- Place safe objects and toys in baby's hand to encourage baby to open and close hands.
- Repetitively show baby your hands closing and opening while saying the corresponding words "Close. Open."
- While changing diaper, bicycle baby's legs to help develop independent leg coordination.

6 -12 MONTHS

THINKING DEVELOPMENT

__Looks and reaches for a specific toy
__Recognizes names for common objects; e.g., cup, ball, toy
__Copies gestures; e.g., "so big" or banging tables
__Looks closely at toys and pictures when object is named
__Looks at and follows moving objects from further distances, such as ball rolling across the floor
__Throws a toy and watches toy to see where it lands
__Removes and puts items back into containers
__Bangs objects together
__Searches for a toy even when toy is not in view

6-12 months Activity Box

THINKING DEVELOPMENT
- Use objects such as pots, pans, and spoons for baby to bang and explore.
- Show baby an object, hide it from sight, and then encourage baby to look for it.
- Name objects and pictures when baby is interacting with them.
- During play, roll balls to encourage wider range of visual tracking.

SOCIAL DEVELOPMENT

__Moves head to follow a voice
__Recognizes familiar faces
__Smiles at self in mirror
__Plays peek-a-boo
__Plays patty cake
__Waves "bye-bye"

6-12 months Activity Box

SOCIAL DEVELOPMENT
- Play games with gestures to imitate; e.g, reaching up arms saying "so big," "patty cake," and wave bye-bye.
- Speak and sing to baby from different areas of the room, to encourage baby to turn and follow the voice.
- Teach blowing kisses.

MORAL DEVELOPMENT

See Age 2

LANGUAGE DEVELOPMENT
__Waves and holds up arms for communication
__Vocalizes to get/keep adult's attention
__Responds to his/her name; e.g., baby Jamie becomes excited when asked, "Where's Jamie?"
__Imitates some adult speech sounds
__Babbles using longer sounds, such as bababababa, mamamama
__Knows/speaks a few words

6-12 months Activity Box

LANGUAGE DEVELOPMENT
- When imitating babbling sounds of baby, repeat with longer patterns such as, "di di di di di di."
- Repeat common words slowly, as baby interacts with them; e.g., "cup" and "ball."
- Use beginner-word flashcards. Consider bilingual cards.
- Encourage baby's verbal communication by responding to all his/her attempts to get your attention.
- Point to self and say, "Mama," and then point to baby and say baby's name to teach infant his/her name.

PHYSICAL DEVELOPMENT
LARGE MUSCLES

__ Sits unsupported for longer periods of time
__ Easily sits up from lying down
__ Turns trunk side to side while sitting
__ Pulls self up on furniture
__ Holds onto chair without leaning
__ Sits down from a standing, supported position
__ Crawls
__ Stands briefly unsupported
__ Begins to take steps when hands held by adult

6-12 months Activity Box

PHYSICAL DEVELOPMENT
Large Muscles
- Sit baby with less support; i.e., first chair and then pillow behind back, as baby gets better at supporting self.
- Place baby in crawling position and slowly move baby's arms and legs in crawling motion. Crawl across floor to show baby.
- Help baby pull self up on furniture to standing position for brief periods of time.
- Help baby to standing position and hold hands while baby takes steps.

---

www.kidsontrackchecklists.com

PHYSICAL DEVELOPMENT
SMALL MUSCLES

__ Picks up objects with thumb and index finger
__ Sticks fingers into holes
__ Transfers toy from one hand to the other hand
__ Crawls around while holding objects
__ Tears paper
__ Plays with musical instruments, such as rattles and drums
__ Uses mouth and hands to learn about environment; e.g., puts toy in mouth while playing
__ Slides, picks up, pushes, and rolls large objects
__ Turns both wheels and cranks
__ Feeds self small pieces of food

6-12 months Activity Box

PHYSICAL DEVELOPMENT
Small Muscles
- Place small pieces of food in front of baby to feed self; e.g., toasted oat cereal.
- Provide play with large and small balls, and musical instruments.
- Give baby a paper towel to tear.

1-2 YEARS

During this stage, go back and assess your child's progress, using the guide in the introduction, to determine if an early intervention evaluation is needed at this point.

THINKING DEVELOPMENT

__Plans out playtime; e.g., gets a toy car and places it on racetrack

__Starts to sort simple shapes into matching groups; e.g., square object in square receptacle

__Orients books and objects right-side up

__Recognizes self in mirror and in photos

__Knows some body parts; e.g., eyes, nose, and mouth

__Completes a beginner puzzle, such as a 2- or 3-piece puzzle

__Imitates routine adult activities; e.g., combing hair, housework

---

1-2 years Activity Box

THINKING DEVELOPMENT
- Use shape-sorting toys.
- Read books with rhymes and stories, and let baby turn pages.
- Look at family photo albums.
- Practice naming a few body parts.
- Do simple puzzles.
- Encourage copycat behavior; e.g., baby wants to clean with broom.
- Encourage baby to make faces in mirror.

SOCIAL DEVELOPMENT

__Begins to play away from parental figure; e.g., explores playground equipment without assistance
__Follows simple directions, such as, "Please pick up the truck and bring it to me."
__Mimics familiar activities; e.g., gives doll a bath
__Shares toys with parent
__Hugs and cuddles with parental figures and others
__Plays alone
__Comforts upset parents or siblings
__Enjoys imitating parents

1-2 years Activity Box

SOCIAL DEVELOPMENT
- Visit playgrounds and allow child to explore in a protected environment.
- Model sharing toys; e.g., switch toys after a few minutes.
- Give simple 2- or 3-step instructions; e.g., "Please get your shoes and bring them to me."
- Encourage baby to play alone for short periods of time.
- Model showing affection and empathy toward family members.

MORAL DEVELOPMENT
See Age 2

LANGUAGE DEVELOPMENT
__Listens to simple rhymes and stories
__Points to a few body parts, if asked; e.g., eyes, nose, and mouth
__Points to pictures in a book, if asked
__Makes many word approximations; e.g., "da" for cat or "nana" for banana
__Categorizes; e.g., says "doggie" for all animals
__Uses more words every month
__By age 18 months, uses about 50 words or approximations of words
__By age 2, uses about 150 words or approximations of words
__Starts using 2-word sentences

1-2 years Activity Box

LANGUAGE DEVELOPMENT
- Give baby 2 choices at snack time and encourage naming the choice; e.g., apple or banana.
- Increase vocabulary development using a book with one photograph on each page and asking baby to point to named object.
- Repeat baby's attempt at simple sentences; e.g., when baby says, "Mo nilk," say slowly, "More milk, please," and encourage baby to repeat. Then give milk.
- Sing the song *Head, Shoulders, Knees and Toes*.
- Ask baby, "Where's baby's (fill in body part)?" (e.g., nose, mouth, eyes, ears, hands, hair, head, feet, elbows, knees, etc.)
- When out of the house with baby, ask, "Do you see a (insert simple object)?" (e.g., tree, bird, dog, etc.)

PHYSICAL DEVELOPMENT
LARGE MUSCLES

__ Walks independently
__ Squats to pick up objects without assistance
__ Begins to run
__ Begins to jump
__ Starts to walk up and down stairs
__ Climbs on furniture
__ Plays with large toys; e.g., pushes and pulls a toy shopping cart
__ Rides alone on a non-pedaled toy
__ Plays catch
__ Bats at a ball with his/her hand
__ Throws a ball a short distance

1-2 years Activity Box

PHYSICAL DEVELOPMENT
Large Muscles
- Place new toys on the floor and encourage baby to squat.
- Provide safe opportunities for climbing, running, and jumping.
- Practice walking up and down stairs.
- Use riding toys; e.g., tricycle without pedals.
- Practice throwing, catching, and batting. Use a laundry basket to help baby's aim.

PHYSICAL DEVELOPMENT
SMALL MUSCLES

__Uses a thick crayon to scribble and draw
__Turns thick pages of a book
__Drinks from a cup
__Starts to feed self with a spoon
__Puts large pegs in pegboard
__Flips light switches and turns door knobs
__Screws lids of containers
__Starts to play with play dough
__Starts to paint with paintbrush
__Plays with water and sand
__Stacks blocks into a tower; i.e., 6 blocks or more
__Pulls apart and reassembles simple objects, such as plastic storage containers, pots, and pans
__Starts to strings a few large beads
__Zips easy zippers

1-2 years Activity Box

PHYSICAL DEVELOPMENT
Small Muscles
- Provide opportunities for art projects using thick crayons, paint, paper, and play dough.
- Give toddler a cup to drink from and a spoon to eat with during meals.
- Practice building block towers.
- Give baby objects to pull apart and put together.
- Provide opportunities to screw lids, use pegs in pegboards, flip switches, and turn door knobs.
- String beads and zip zippers.
- Put a toy in each hand to promote independent hand manipulation.

2-3 YEARS

THINKING DEVELOPMENT

__Concepts grow rapidly; e.g., family, weather, and familiar places
__Concepts are in the present tense
__Thinking is self-centered; i.e., "Everyone thinks the way I do."
__Learns and repeats common sounds, such as "moo" and "vroom vroom"
__Asks for things using words and gestures
__Enjoys taking things apart; e.g., a cabinet of pots, or toys with bells and whistles
__Counts to at least 10
__Names a few body parts; e.g., eyes, nose, mouth, hand, foot, and head
__Names familiar people from photographs
__Points to familiar things when wants something; e.g., points at a cup when thirsty
__Groups objects by shape, color, and size
__Matches simple pictures
__Identifies a few colors when asked; e.g., "Which car is blue?"
__Copies drawing lines and gluing paper; e.g., watches an adult draw a circle and glue on eyes, a nose, and a mouth, and then copies
__Forms blocks into trains and towers

SOCIAL DEVELOPMENT

__Explores away from caregiver, acting independently; e.g., climbs on playground equipment with caregiver nearby

__Desires power and independence, but still wants caregiver present

__Plays for a few minutes next to other children

__Shows affection when playing with familiar children

__Understands what is "mine" and what is "his/hers"

__Enjoys imitating others

__Begins to take turns when playing a game

MORAL DEVELOPMENT

__Obeys rules to avoid punishment and consequences; e.g., shares a toy because she/he doesn't want to lose the toy

__Views others' points-of-view as being the same as own point-of-view; e.g., "I like pizza so everyone likes pizza."

__Says, "Please," when making a request

__Says, "Thank you," when receiving something

__Learns vocabulary words associated with emotions, such as shy, happy, angry

2-3 years Activity Box

THINKING DEVELOPMENT
- Talk about basic concepts; e.g., home, school, and seasons.
- Play matching and sorting games.
- Ask toddler to help match socks.
- Name common sounds, colors, and textures, asking toddler to repeat.
- Continue to point to and name objects/people in books, encouraging toddler to repeat.
- Practice counting to 10, singing the alphabet, and naming more body parts.
- Model drawing lines and pasting paper.

SOCIAL DEVELOPMENT
- Have play dates with other children.
- Model turn taking, using a kitchen timer to encourage fairness in sharing.

MORAL DEVELOPMENT
- Model saying "please" and "thank you."
- Explain simple rules; e.g., "If you hit your sister, you will go to your room for 5 minutes."
- Label emotions as child experiences them; e.g., "I see that you are angry."

LANGUAGE DEVELOPMENT

__Listens to longer stories

__Follows a 2-step direction: "Get your shoes and go to the chair."

__Gains 5 to 6 new vocabulary words a day

__Uses words or approximations of words for everything; e.g., "nil" for milk consistently

__Uses at least four words in a sentence

__Pronounces words more clearly; most speech is understood by strangers

__Understands opposites, such as big vs. little, up vs. down

PHYSICAL DEVELOPMENT
LARGE MUSCLES

__Pushes and pulls wheeled objects with ease

__Runs with coordination

__Walks up and down stairs confidently

__Jumps in place using both feet together

__Hops on one foot briefly

__Stands on one foot briefly

__Walks backwards briefly

__Tiptoes

__Kicks a ball

__Throws and catches a large ball from a short distance

www.kidsontrackchecklists.com

2-3 years Activity Box

LANGUAGE DEVELOPMENT
- Point out opposites; e.g., big vs. little, up vs. down.
- Continue to give 2- and 3-step directions.
- Give toddler opportunities to say many sentences without interruption.
- Read stories for longer periods of time to increase attention span.
- Model using longer sentences with proper grammar and introduce new vocabulary words.

PHYSICAL DEVELOPMENT

Large Muscles
- Encourage pushing carts, running, jumping in place, balancing, and walking backwards.
- Promote using the stairs.
- Practice kicking and throwing balls.
- Play hop scotch to encourage hopping on one foot.
- Teach line dancing to develop walking in different directions.

PHYSICAL DEVELOPMENT
SMALL MUSCLES

__Uses utensils and drinks from a cup independently
__Brushes teeth with help
__Dresses and undresses with help
__Washes hands independently
__Makes a few paintbrush strokes when painting
__Uses play dough and clay
__Plays with water and sand
__Folds and rips paper
__Unbuttons and buttons
__Screws and unscrews lids
__Latches gate or other latches
__Strings smaller beads and shoelaces; e.g., uses yarn and beads to string a necklace
__Uses stacking and nesting toys properly
__Places pegs in pegboards correctly
__Holds book right-side up and turns book pages
__Grips a pencil with whole hand and may change grips often
__Draws a few basic shapes; e.g., circles, triangles, squares
__Begins to use child scissors
__Uses toy hammer and pours liquid from container to container with good accuracy

www.kidsontrackchecklists.com

2-3 years Activity Box

PHYSICAL DEVELOPMENT

Small Muscles

- Provide opportunity to use play dough, clay, sand, water.
- Use containers to pour water from one to the other during bath time.
- Encourage using a spoon and a cup during meals.
- Model holding a book and turning pages correctly, asking toddler to repeat.
- Give opportunities to button and unbutton, latch and unlatch, string smaller beads, and hit small objects with a toy hammer.
- Using an old shoe, help practice shoe lacing.
- Use nesting blocks; i.e., ones that stack inside and also can be used to build a tower.
- Use crayons, pencils, paintbrushes, and child-proof scissors.
- Encourage washing hands, brushing teeth, and dressing independently.

3-4 YEARS

THINKING DEVELOPMENT

__Builds background knowledge; e.g., seasons, lifecycle of a butterfly
__Repeats common nursery rhymes, such as *The Itsy Bitsy Spider*
__Does finger play; e.g., *Where is Thumbkin?*
__Reads own name
__Reads some environmental print; e.g., "Exit" sign
__Begins to learn alphabet
__Names some colors, such as red, blue, yellow, green, orange
__Knows basic shapes: triangle, circle, square, etc.
__Classifies by texture: hot vs. cold, wet vs. dry, soft vs. hard, etc.
__Groups objects by shape, color, size, and texture
__Completes simple patterns; e.g., red block, blue block, red block. "What comes next?"
__Holds up correct number of fingers when asked his/her age
__Recognizes written numbers; i.e., 1-10
__Counts up to 20
__Uses 1:1 matching when counting objects; e.g., when the child is given 5 buttons, he/she points to each button and assigns a number, 1 through 5, in the correct order
__Completes easy puzzles: 10 to 15 pieces

3-4 years Activity Box

THINKING DEVELOPMENT

- Practice counting on fingers and writing numbers.
- Ask child to name objects by color, shape, size, and texture.
- Put different textured items in a bag and have child name them.
- Sing, and use cards, puzzles, or bath toys to teach the alphabet.
- Sing, together, common nursery rhymes and finger plays, such as *The Itsy Bitsy Spider*.
- Practice counting objects one by one, and complete easy puzzles.
- Display child's name to practice reading.
- Ask child to sort objects by category; e.g., shape, wet vs. dry, small vs. big.
- Use beads or blocks to make simple patterns, such as red, blue, red, blue.
- Point out differences in the seasons: leaves fall in autumn, snow falls in winter, etc.

SOCIAL DEVELOPMENT

__Explores environment confidently; e.g., jumps, runs, throws, and slides without assistance
__Displays initiative during play; e.g., will ask to ride on bike
__Takes turns when playing a game
__Begins pretend play; e.g., playing house
__Seeks out independence

3-4 years Activity Box

SOCIAL DEVELOPMENT
- Find large, safe areas where child can run and explore.
- Encourage pretend play; e.g., acting out a visit to the doctor.
- Play board games to develop turn taking.

MORAL DEVELOPMENT

__Obeys orders for own needs and desires; e.g., will be quiet for a cookie
__Reasoning is reward-based: "What do I get out of it?"
__Interested in others only to further own interests, e.g., will share a toy for a lollipop
__Says "excuse me" when trying to pass others
__Names emotion and identifies cause; e.g., "I'm happy because I have a new toy."

3-4 years Activity Box
MORAL DEVELOPMENT
- Encourage saying, "excuse me" when appropriate, in addition to "please" and "thank you."
- Offer immediate rewards for positive behavior; e.g., "If you wait for your turn quietly, you can pick the next game."
- Encourage naming cause of an emotion; e.g., "Why are you angry?"

---

www.kidsontrackchecklists.com

LANGUAGE DEVELOPMENT

__ Answers simple questions, such as, "Who is that?" or, "What do you want?"

__ Talks about current activities; e.g., what happened at school

__ Speech is understood by others

__ Follows many-step directions: 2 to 3 steps

__ Talks easily, using many sentences

__ Talks without stuttering; e.g., child no longer says "He went went went to the pa pa park."

3-4 years Activity Box

LANGUAGE DEVELOPMENT

- Have conversations about everything in child's environment, using who, what, where, when, and why questions.
- Allow ample time for child to speak multiple sentences.
- Allow ample time for child to complete sentences to avoid interrupting child in the middle of a sentence.
- Acknowledge child by looking and listening when he/she is speaking.

PHYSICAL DEVELOPMENT
LARGE MUSCLES

__Claps and sways to music
__Jumps longer distances
__Balances well while walking on a beam
__Runs with ease
__Runs backward
__Pedals a bicycle
__Stands briefly on one foot without support
__Hops briefly on one foot
__Throws overhand and catches a ball at short distances
__Throws a small ball overhand
__Kicks and dribbles a ball for short distances

3-4 years Activity Box

PHYSICAL DEVELOPMENT

Large Muscles

- Play child-friendly music and encourage dancing and jumping.
- Model walking on a beam, jumping large distances, standing on one foot, hopping, and tiptoeing, asking child to repeat.
- Provide opportunities for running and bike riding.
- Encourage kicking a soccer ball, both still and rolling.
- Help practice throwing a ball in the air and to a target.
- Play tag.

PHYSICAL DEVELOPMENT
SMALL MUSCLES

__ Rolls and pats play dough or clay
__ Uses basic art materials, such as crayons, pencils, paintbrushes, child scissors
__ Uses correct grip when holding a pencil; i.e., thumb, index, and middle fingers
__ Copies and traces basic shapes
__ Cuts with child-safe scissors
__ Builds more complex structures with blocks; e.g., pyramid
__ Puts pegs in a pegboard
__ Strings beads
__ Copies some alphabet letters; e.g., H, E, T
__ Dresses and undresses independently
__ Puts on shoes and brushes teeth independently

3-4 years Activity Box

PHYSICAL DEVELOPMENT
Small Muscles

- Model rolling play dough and patting it flat, asking child to imitate.
- Model appropriate grip on a pencil, using thumb, index, and middle fingers, asking child to imitate.
- Draw circles and lines for child to copy.
- Practice tracing basic shapes using templates.
- Trace alphabet letters and numbers using templates.
- Use smaller toy pegs and string smaller beads.
- Build more complex block towers and bridges.
- Allow child ample time to dress/undress, brush teeth, and put on shoes.

4-5 YEARS

THINKING DEVELOPMENT
__Talks about the past
__Begins to learn alphabet sounds
__Reads more basic words
__Masters 1-1 matching; i.e., can count out 10 crayons one at a time
__Sequences simple pictures; e.g., plants a seed and then waters ground; then a flower grows
__Recognizes numbers 10-20
__Counts to 20+
__Knows more colors; e.g., purple, pink
__Knows more 2-dimensional shapes; e.g., rectangle, oval
__Compares groups by size, length, amount, color, and shape
__Completes more complex patterns; e.g., blue, blue, red, yellow, blue, blue, red, yellow
__Identifies items by touch; e.g., can find the clock in toy box without looking

SOCIAL DEVELOPMENT
__Plays in a group
__Pretend play is more developed; e.g., saving a princess from a castle
__Pretend play involves more turn taking with peers
__Sharing and turn taking with peers happens more frequently

4-5 years Activity Box

THINKING DEVELOPMENT

- Play board games and model moving the piece on each space while counting, to teach 1:1 matching.
- Use alphabet letters with pictures to teach alphabet sounds.
- Count to higher numbers and show written numbers.
- Read books with 1-2 sentences on each page and point to each word while reading.
- Ask child about colors, shapes, and different textures in the environment.
- Play sorting games that classify by size, length, amount, color, shape, and texture.
- Create more complex color patterns with beads, blocks, or drawing materials; e.g., red, red, blue, blue, yellow, and repeat.
- After reading, say, in simple sentences, what happened in the beginning, middle, and end of the story.

4-5 years Activity Box

SOCIAL DEVELOPMENT
- Add props for pretend play; e.g., setting the table, making a meal in the toy kitchen, and eating it.
- Model taking turns with objects and toys during pretend play; e.g., "I'll make the eggs and you make the toast. Then we will switch."
- Some of the time, set up pretend play and then leave the room to encourage child to pretend independently; e.g., set table and leave while child pretends to cook.

MORAL DEVELOPMENT

__Begins to see others' needs, but still looks out for self first

__Shows some empathy; e.g., comforts peers when they are crying

__Displays manners more automatically; e.g., every time the child asks, he or she says, "Please...?"

__Understands relationship between hard work and reward; e.g., having a job earns money to buy what you want

4-5 years Activity Box

MORAL DEVELOPMENT
- When child has a conflict, say the words you want child to say; e.g., "I want a turn with that toy when you are done," and encourage, without demanding, child to repeat.
- Watch and reward for good manners during child's interactions; e.g., saying "please," "thank you," "excuse me," and "I'm sorry."
- Provide a list of chores with rewards; e.g., stickers or allowance.

LANGUAGE DEVELOPMENT

__Understands conversations at home and in other environments ✓

__Listens to a short story displaying good attention span; e.g., answers basic questions about the story ✓

__Pronounces most sounds properly ✓

__Adds more detail during conversation ✓

__Expresses self clearly to peers and adults

__Stays on the topic when telling a story

4-5 years Activity Box

LANGUAGE DEVELOPMENT

- After reading a story, ask child basic questions using who, what, where, when, and why.
- When child is telling a story, check for clarity, details, and staying on topic; e.g., explaining a class trip to the farm.
- Ask child simple questions about experiences in the recent past; e.g., an outing from 2 days ago.

PHYSICAL DEVELOPMENT
LARGE MUSCLES

__Masters tiptoeing and walking forward and backward on a beam
__Hops and skips
__Pumps legs on a swing
__Forward rolls easily
__Runs around obstacles; e.g., runs around cones spaced apart in a line
__Pedals a tricycle well
__Begins jumping rope
__Climbs up ladder and goes down slide independently
__Catches ball with hands and chest

4-5 years Activity Box
PHYSICAL DEVELOPMENT
Large Muscles
- Take child to playgrounds and/or gym classes to practice basic skills.
- Play freeze dance.
- Use equipment to increase development, such as jump rope, tricycle, swing, toy ladder with slide, and various sized balls.

---

www.kidsontrackchecklists.com

PHYSICAL DEVELOPMENT
SMALL MUSCLES

__Buttons and zips/unzips without assistance
__Uses key to open locks
__Uses screws and bolts to screw/unscrew
__Maintains good eye contact with a moving ball
__Colors within the lines
__Does simple weaving
__Traces and cuts using simple shapes or picture stencils
__Draws a person with a few body parts; e.g., head, legs, eyes
__Traces own hand
__Draws lines to connect dots
__Copies own name
__Cuts a straight line with child scissors

4-5 years Activity Box

PHYSICAL DEVELOPMENT
Small Muscles
- Check for correct grip when child uses writing materials.
- Allow child ample time to assemble own clothing; e.g., zipping and buttoning.
- Play with toys that lock/unlock and have screws and bolts.
- Give child activity pages from books or the computer, with dot-to-dots and coloring, tracing, and cutting pages.
- Give blank paper and encourage drawing family members and tracing own hand.

5-7 YEARS

THINKING DEVELOPMENT

__ Talks about the future
__ Begins abstract thought, such as words on a page are symbols that represent the spoken story
__ Identifies rhymes; e.g., "cat" rhymes with "hat"
__ Reads picture books and grade-level chapter books ✓
__ Understands story elements, such as characters, plot, problems, and solutions
__ Reads basic color names ✓
__ Starts beginner writing that imitates adult activities; e.g., making shopping lists or writing short stories and songs
__ Recognizes and spells first and last name ✓
__ Writes letters and numbers correctly
__ Responds to literature in writing, using a few simple sentences; e.g., teacher reads a story and child writes a response ✓
__ By age 7, writes simple sentences, mostly spelled correctly
__ By age 7, names a topic and can write about it; e.g., "*My summer vacation*"
__ Identifies and predicts patterns; e.g., red, red, blue, red, red…
__ Sorts items by at least 2 descriptors; e.g., purple triangle ✓
__ Lines up items in size order ✓

www.kidsontrackchecklists.com

THINKING DEVELOPMENT (continued)
__Recognizes numbers to 100
__Counts to 100
__By age 7, writes numbers to 100
__Understands basic mathematical operations; i.e., addition and subtraction
__Skip counts by 10's, 5's, 2's
__Understands how to use a calendar
__Understands how to use a ruler and a measuring cup
__Reads, writes, and labels a basic graph; e.g., a bar graph
__Knows grade-level geometry; e.g., 2-D shapes, such as hexagons and parallelograms
__Identifies and knows the value of 4 basic coins
__Tells time to the hour and half hour on analog and digital clocks
__Completes easy puzzles
__Plays basic card games; e.g., *Go Fish*

5-7 years Activity Box

THINKING DEVELOPMENT
Reading
- Read environmental print with child wherever you are; e.g., reading a menu or signs and billboards.
- Read a variety of books with child every day; e.g., rhyming books, or stories with different genres, such as fables, science, or poetry.
- Provide leveled books to increase child's reading development.
- Point out story elements while reading; e.g., characters, plots, problems, and solution.
- Show examples of how reading and writing are useful in everyday activities; e.g., grocery lists, songs, own name.

www.kidsontrackchecklists.com

5-7 years Activity Box

THINKING DEVELOPMENT
Writing
- Practice reading and spelling basic sight words that break common spelling rules (about 100 of them); e.g., "love," "the," "one," etc.
- Practice correct formation of numbers and letters, as well as correct spacing of letters, words, sentences, and paragraphs.
- Write about life experiences, having child add more sentences with more details over time; e.g., class trip to the zoo or summer vacation.
- Practice correct grammar and punctuation.

5-7 years Activity Box

THINKING DEVELOPMENT

Math

- Practice correct number formation to 100, pointing out patterns; e.g., 10, 20, 30, and so on.
- Count and form groups using common objects; e.g., pennies and buttons, and add a number sentence; e.g., 2+3=5.
- Use a daily calendar with child to learn days, weeks, months, years, seasons, and weather.
- Involve child in simple cooking projects to practice measurement and fractions.
- Measure simple objects, such as an arm or a glass.
- Play shape games; e.g., "How many rectangles are in this room?"
- Use the four basic coins and a dollar bill to teach the names and values.
- Practice using both a digital and an analog clock to teach time.
- Do more advanced puzzles and play age-level card and board games.

SOCIAL DEVELOPMENT

__Influenced more by peers and teachers, and less by parents
__Wants to create things and feel successful
__Seeks praise from adults to feel good about self and abilities
__Interested in conversations with others
__Interacts more with peers during play with less playing side by side
__Has more advanced pretend play, for longer periods of time

5-7 years Activity Box

SOCIAL DEVELOPMENT

- Try out a variety of activities with child and give praise often; e.g., sports, music, and art.
- Discuss with child, and ask questions about, daily activities and family plans, to develop good conversational skills.
- Allow time for play with same-age children outside of school.
- Encourage more advanced pretend play; e.g., pirates seeking treasure.

MORAL DEVELOPMENT

__Believes rules are laws, and doesn't question them; e.g., waiting in line for a movie
__Reasons that rules are for everyone and should not be broken; e.g., everyone has to eat in the kitchen
__Empathy toward others develops; e.g., will help a friend in need

---

5-7 years Activity Box

MORAL DEVELOPMENT

- Point out positive and negative behavior in others, as a model for child.
- Create a few basic rules for child and reasonable consequences if they are broken; e.g., "Keep your hands and your feet on your body, or there will be a 5-minute 'time out'."
- Encourage empathy toward others; e.g., child gets a bandage for a friend with a scraped knee.

---

www.kidsontrackchecklists.com

LANGUAGE DEVELOPMENT

__ Gains new words learned and spoken daily
__ Tells more advanced stories and has more complex conversations; e.g., provides more details and remains on topic
__ Listens to longer stories; answers simple questions
__ Understands that the text on a page corresponds with the spoken word during story time
__ Makes predictions within stories; e.g., answers, "What will happen next?"
__ Follows complex commands; e.g., 4 to 5 steps

5-7 years Activity Box

LANGUAGE DEVELOPMENT

- Have detailed conversations about child's experiences in the recent past, present, and near future.
- Read aloud stories to child without pictures and ask a few basic questions to clarify understanding.
- When child is reading a story, stop at a particular point and ask, "What will happen next?"
- After child reads a story, ask the child to retell the story pointing out the beginning, middle, and end.

PHYSICAL DEVELOPMENT
LARGE MUSCLES

__Hops and skips farther distances
__Rides a bike, first with training wheels, then without
__Does push-ups and sit-ups
__Walks down stairs while carrying objects
__Runs well through obstacle courses
__Sprints short distances
__Marches to music
__Skips, jumps rope, and roller skates
__Uses hands instead of arms when catching and throwing balls
__Climbs and jumps about 3-4 feet; e.g., the height of a table
__Displays coordinated complex body movements, such as plays tag, crawls through playground tunnels, and rolls down a hill
__Maneuvers on monkey bars

5-7 years Activity Box

PHYSICAL DEVELOPMENT
Large Muscles
- Practice hopping, skipping, jumping, walking on tip toes, and balancing.
- Set up obstacle courses and encourage practicing moving through the obstacles and sprinting.
- Ride a bike with training wheels and eventually remove training wheels.
- Practice pushups, sit-ups, and dancing to music.

PHYSICAL DEVELOPMENT
SMALL MUSCLES

__Uses right or left hand predominantly
__Uses pegs for pegboard designs
__Ties shoes independently
__Cuts out more complex shapes and simple pictures using child scissors
__Draws a person with most body parts
__Ties and unties knots
__Cuts food well

5-7 years Activity Box
PHYSICAL DEVELOPMENT
Small Muscles
- Do projects using a variety of classroom tools; e.g., scissors.
- Cut out shapes and pictures using paper and/or cloth.
- Draw shapes and people with body parts.
- Practice tying shoes and knots and cutting food.
- Build more complex block structures and pegboard designs.
- Practice throwing, catching, and kicking different size balls.

7-11 YEARS

THINKING DEVELOPMENT

__Develops more sophisticated abstract thought; e.g., "There is more than one way to solve a problem."
__Makes more predictions about the future; e.g., "What will you see on our trip on Friday?"
__Relationships have literal meanings; e.g., "He is in my family because he lives in my house."
__Uses familiar situations to problem solve and create new concepts; e.g., child is sweating and decides to take off his /her jacket
__Reads grade-level chapter books, with fluency and understanding
__Reads and understands grade-level subject areas, such as science and social studies
__Writes about literature using several sentences and then paragraphs
__By age 11, develops understanding that others think differently and have other perspectives
__Draws simple maps of familiar places
__Develops understanding of relationships within a group; e.g., girls vs. boys, hair color, eye color
__Classifies objects and draws comparisons, such as smaller vs. larger, lighter vs. darker, easier vs. harder
__Understands higher-level math operations; i.e., multiplication and division

THINKING DEVELOPMENT (continued)

__Knows grade-level geometry; e.g., 3-D shapes such as cube and sphere
__Understands and uses money
__Adds and subtracts money
__Records elapsed time, such as the length of an activity
__Understands equal parts; i.e., fractions
__By age 11, calculates fractions

7-11 years Activity Box

THINKING DEVELOPMENT
Reasoning
- Ask questions about past events and prediction questions about the future; e.g., "Where did we go last spring vacation? What will we see when we go back there next week?"
- Point out similarities and differences in child's world; e.g, relationships within a family or differences between animals.
- Model differences as positive; e.g., people's different perspectives or physical attributes.

7-11 years Activity Box

THINKING DEVELOPMENT
Reading
- Check that reading is on grade level, as determined by assessment tools used by schools.
- Read a new chapter book every week, for pleasure.
- Read nonfiction books, such as science or sports, and check for understanding.
- Encourage researching new topics of interest; e.g., trips to the library and reading periodicals.

7-11 years Activity Box

THINKING DEVELOPMENT
Writing
- Encourage writing multiple paragraphs on a topic and responding, in writing, to a variety of genres, such as adventure, sports, history, and poetry.
- Keep a journal; e.g., vacations and summer break.
- Check that spelling is improving all the time.
- Build vocabulary by writing a word on one side of an index card and the definition on the other side; e.g., science and social studies vocabulary words.

7-11 years Activity Box

THINKING DEVELOPMENT

Math

- Use higher-level math operations in everyday life; e.g., "If we want 3 balloons and they are $2.00 each, how much money do we need?"
- Build speed and automaticity of math facts using flash cards; i.e., addition, subtraction, multiplication, and division.
- Model and engage child in using money to understand value, adding, and making change.
- Discuss time and predict elapsed time; e.g., "What time is it now? We have to be at the park in 2 hours. What time will it be then?"
- Use everyday items such as pizza or a cake to explain fractions and geometry.
- Complete grade-level activity books, with child, to improve math skills; e.g., fractions and geometry.
- Encourage drawing maps; e.g., treasure hunt, rooms in house, places in the community.

SOCIAL DEVELOPMENT

__Expands social world; e.g., develops relationships with peers and teachers

__Seeks ability to measure up to others' standards; e.g., peer pressures

__Feels good about self and own abilities when successful; e.g., good grades in school or excelling in sports

__Uses conversation to further friendships

__Takes turns and shares easily

7-11 years Activity Box

SOCIAL DEVELOPMENT

- Find activities that make child feel successful, such as sports, martial arts, dance, or music.
- Give praise for desired behaviors; e.g., child comes in and hangs up coat.
- Discuss "peer pressure" as a part of life and read age-appropriate books on the topic with child.
- Allow ample time for child to socialize and develop friendships with same-age children in a safe environment.
- Discuss hard topics with children; e.g., puberty and drug addiction.

MORAL DEVELOPMENT

__Becomes aware of others' different perspectives; e.g., can put self in "someone else's shoes"

__Believes in treating others as he/she wishes to be treated

__Understands that rules exist for the betterment of society; e.g., "If I break a law, everyone would," which is not good for society

__Bases moral decisions first on seeking approval from others, then on social norms

---

7-11 years Activity Box

MORAL DEVELOPMENT
- Give praise when child exhibits positive behaviors toward others; e.g., helps a friend or displays good manners.
- When child is having a conflict with a peer, encourage predicting how he or she would feel, to help solve the problem.
- Encourage empathy toward child's social circle, and eventually toward society.

LANGUAGE DEVELOPMENT

__Listens to and understands stories without pictures
__Learns new vocabulary words every week
__Converses for longer periods of time

PHYSICAL DEVELOPMENT

__Performs activities for longer periods of time; e.g., biking, skating, catching, jumping rope
__Develops skills and interests in sports, dance, and musical instruments
__Improves coordination
__Improves control of own speed; e.g., bike riding and skiing
__Improves performance skills in areas of interest; e.g., throw a baseball with greater accuracy

7-11 years Activity Box

LANGUAGE DEVELOPMENT
- Read age-appropriate novels aloud to child, in small parts, and ask basic questions to check for understanding.
- Model using advanced vocabulary words during conversation.
- Give child ample time to speak in order to express thoughts and desires.

PHYSICAL DEVELOPMENT
- Find and engage in weekly physical activities that the child enjoys; e.g., organized sports, gym, or martial arts.
- Try out team activities.
- Expose child to a variety of music, musical instruments, and arts.

EARLY INTERVENTION SERVICES
(A through M)

Alabama	(334) 293-7166
Alaska	(907) 269-8442
Arizona	(602) 532-9960
Arkansas	(501) 682-8156
California	(800) 404-5900
Colorado	(303) 866-7657
Connecticut	(860) 418-6147
Delaware	(302) 255-9135
Florida	(850) 245-4444
Georgia	(404) 657-2762
Hawaii	(808) 594-0006
Idaho	(208) 334-5523
Illinois	(217) 782-1981
Indiana	(317) 233-9229
Iowa	(515) 281-5437
Kansas	(785) 296-6135
Kentucky	(270) 746-9941
Louisiana	(225) 355-4461
Maine	(207) 624-6660
Maryland	(443) 275-1663
Massachusetts	(617) 624-5901
Michigan	(248) 559-5820
Minnesota	(218) 284-3800
Mississippi	(601) 576-7427
Missouri	(573) 751-3559
Montana	(406) 444-2995

www.kidsontrackchecklists.com

EARLY INTERVENTION SERVICES
(N through W)

Nebraska	(402) 471-9329
Nevada	(775) 688-1341
New Hampshire	(603) 271-5122
New Jersey	(609) 538-0025
New Mexico	(505) 476-8975
New York	(518) 473-7016
North Carolina	(919) 707-5520
North Dakota	(701) 328-8936
Ohio	(800) 755-4769
Oklahoma	(405) 521-4155
Oregon	(541) 312-1947
Pennsylvania	(800) 692-7288
Rhode Island	(401) 462-0318
South Carolina	(803) 898-0784
South Dakota	(605) 773-4478
Tennessee	(615) 253-2589
Texas	(800) 628-5115
Utah	(801) 584-8441
Vermont	(802) 241-3622
Virginia	(804) 786-3710
Washington	(206) 263-9061
West Virginia	(304) 558-5388
Wisconsin	(262) 658-9500
Wyoming	(307) 777-7115

Please note that phone numbers are subject to change.

Acknowledgments

Michele Fitzsimmons

The inspiration for this book has always been my three greatest gifts, my sons. I want to thank my loving husband, Tim, for his dedication to our family. To my mother, Lorraine, thank you for all your love and support. To my father, Arnie, thank you for your ideas. I want to acknowledge my family and friends, whose enthusiasm and insight influenced the success of this project. To my partner and good friend, Theresa, thank you for your tireless effort and for bringing this book to a whole new level. I want to recognize a special teacher, Nevine, from whom I've learned to march the march to find the magic.

M. Theresa Bromley, PA-C

Approximately two years ago, Michele asked me if I would be interested in helping her with this project. Given my love of children and of practicing pediatrics, I jumped at the opportunity. In the beginning, we did not realize the enormity of our project. So, to my children, thank you for understanding when mommy was working on her "other" job. I also would like to thank my husband, Michael, my parents, Nanette and Darrell, and Paulina and Viviana, for providing me with the time to work on this book. I could never have done this without you. Finally, I send a heartfelt thank you to our friends for all their support and encouragement.

Together, we send a special thank you to Alexis and James for doing a great job illustrating our book cover. To Kyra Bromley and Don Hunnewell, thank you for helping resolve our technical difficulties because we could not have finished the book without you. Finally, to Raquel Lorena Morales, Carol Kalfian, Denise Ciraldo, and Oscar Schachter, we appreciate all of your contributions to this book.

www.kidsontrackchecklists.com

i) grouping and sorting
ii) patterning
iii) Jumping, hopping, balancing on one foot, cycling
iv) throwing + catching
v) sequencing
vi) spontaneous conversation
vii) hand writing
viii) basic story telling

NB   Role play games.
     board game playing.

   Needs to go to a gym class.

Tennis set   Hoopla?
skittles.   cricket set?